YOU COMPLETE VIRGO 2023 PERSONAL HOROSCOPE

Monthly Astrological Prediction Forecast Readings of Every Zodiac Astrology Sun Star Signs- Love, Romance, Money, Finances, Career, Health, Travel, Spirituality.

Iris Quinn

Alpha Zuriel Publishing

Your Complete Virgo 2023 Personal Horoscope/ Iris Quinn. -- 1st ed.

We are born at a specific time and place, and, like vintage years of wine, we have the characteristics of the year and season in which we are born. Astrology claims nothing more.
— CARL JUNG

CONTENTS

CHAPTER ONE

VIRGO PROFILE

Constellation: Virgo

Zodiac symbol: Maiden

Date: August 22 – September 22

Zodiac element: Earth

Zodiac quality: Mutable

Greatest Compatibility: Cancer and Pisces

Sign ruler: Mercury

Day: Wednesday

Color: Beige and Grey

Birthstone: Sapphire

VIRGO TRAITS

- Must feel useful.
- Has a quick solution for everything
- Judgmental but well-intended.
- Superior spatial awareness
- A million thoughts per second

PERSONALITY OF VIRGO

Virgos are often modest individuals. They want to be recognized for their achievements, but they don't require spectacular displays of gratitude to feel worthwhile. They're like little geniuses. They pay attention to the subtleties. When Virgo's toothbrush is moved even a centimeter, they notice.

Virgos are self-conscious about their imperfections. They understand that their actions have repercussions and that they can be accountable for their own misery at times. This is why they frequently say things like "It's my fault" and "I did this to myself."

Virgos are the exact incarnation of the mediaeval philosopher who dwells in a sterile cell, never opening the door for fear of exposing the shambles within. "In order to save myself from myself, I must first destroy myself," their motto says. They desire a pristine, clean existence.

They must be the best in order to feel worthy of their existence. They can become so preoccupied with their own ideal of perfection that they lose touch with their actual desires. They suppress their emotions by locking them up in order to achieve impassivity.

They can appear lot more sensible than they actually are. Their emotions are typically a mystery to them. They have a lot of feelings, but they don't know how to express them. They can only express the ineffable through dry sarcasm.

WEAKNESSES OF VIRGO

Virgos are perfectionists by nature. Cleaning freaks, they are well-known for their meticulousness. They can see patterns where none exist. They can be picky and too critical.

True, Virgos are particular, but that doesn't always imply that they preserve neat spaces. Their peculiarities and behaviors may not often correspond to traditional notions of cleanliness. They may live in a Tasmanian devil-style dust storm ruin while enforcing a "no shoes in the house" or "no outside clothing on the bed" restriction. Their home may appear cluttered, but they know where everything is. Everything has a purpose. Virgos prefer to be in order, but they prioritize their service orientation over their own comfort. This can indicate that a Virgo is too preoccupied with improving the lives of those around them to devote much time and effort to meeting their own needs. They are rarely driven by self-interest.

Virgos are brilliant as well, but because of their reclusive nature, they sometimes have difficulty expressing themselves. Talking to a Virgo may feel like you're hovering on the surface of life, with no idea what they're feeling deep inside or thinking. Their emphasis on thinking and ideas may appear to be a mask for a lack of emotional depth. In reality, they are a fortress within a fortress—the epitome of self-containment. Virgos will be open to everything you have to offer, but they may not see the point of impulsively excavating themselves for the sake of others.

RELATIONSHIP COMPATIBILITY WITH VIRGO

Based only on their Sun signs, this is how Virgo interacts with others. These are the compatibility interpretations for all 12 potential Virgo combinations. This is a limited and insufficient method of determining compatibility.

However, Sun-sign compatibility remains the foundation for overall harmony in a relationship.

The general rule is that yin and yang do not get along. Yin complements yin, and yang complements yang. While yin and yang partnerships can be successful, they require more effort. Earth and water zodiac signs are both Yin. Yang is represented by the fire and air zodiac signs.

Aries and Virgo

This is a difficult connection to maintain. Both Virgo and Aries have powerful personalities, yet their ambitions are totally different. Aries is an action-oriented mindset, whereas Virgo is always analyzing and shredding any situation that happens. Aries has to progress, but Virgo is impeding him with judgments and reprimands. Maybe, with a lot of effort, they'll discover a way.

Taurus and Virgo

Virgo and Taurus have a wonderful partnership that has enormous potential to become steady and dependable. Virgo and Taurus are two earth signs with numerous similarities. They have similar tastes: they both enjoy planning initiatives, bettering themselves, cultivating their minds, analyzing expenses and household demands, and so on. Of course, they must be careful not to get stuck in a rut.

Gemini and Virgo

Because of the diverse ways they express their natures, a partnership between Virgo and Gemini would be too hard to sustain and become solid. Both Virgo and Gemini are mutable signs ruled by Mercury, yet they work on separate wavelengths. Virgo is an earthly sign, while Gemini is an air sign. Gemini personifies dispersion and unpredictability. Virgo, on the other hand, does not leave anything to chance: it examines its steps indefinitely. This attribute is a hefty load for Gemini to bear on a daily basis.

Cancer and Virgo

A partnership between Virgo and Cancer can be quite rewarding if both members manage to provide room for each other without suffocating each other. Many of their requirements are shared by Virgo and Cancer: they will seek affection, assist each other in difficult times, feel safe, and share lots of hugs and pampering. Virgo must be careful not to slip into the habit of continual criticism.

Leo and Virgo

A Virgo and Leo partnership will require a lot of effort. Virgo is an overly fastidious and critical sign, and Leo will be reluctant to allow their partner point out their flaws. On the other hand, Leo requires regular flattery, and providing such flattery is not a quality present in the area of Virgo. If this partnership is to succeed, Virgo and Leo must get to know each other thoroughly and offer a few inches.

Virgo and Virgo

A relationship between two Virgos will be difficult since each will strive to dominate the other. Because

Virgos are precise and detail-oriented, they will critique one another's activities in order to keep control of the relationship. Neither has the ability to relax and minimize their mental stiffness. It's quite difficult.

Libra and Virgo

A Virgo and Libra relationship is difficult but not impossible. To ensure the success of their partnership, Virgo and Libra should try to reach a compromise. Virgo has to stop being so judgmental. Libra should try to curb its seductive tendencies because Virgo is extremely devoted and will not accept inappropriate behavior in the partnership.

Scorpio and Virgo

A Virgo-Scorpion partnership can be very rewarding. Scorpio will be pleased with its adored Virgo since Virgo will appreciate Scorpio's accomplishments and will not be as critical as other signs. Scorpio's temper tantrums and feelings of jealousy will be handled well by Virgo, who has great analytical skills.

Sagittarius and Virgo

A partnership between Virgo and Sagittarius is nearly impossible to sustain. They are so diametrically opposed that they can barely get to know each other. A volatile, changing, unstable, and reckless individual will not be tolerated by Virgo. Sagittarius will take off rapidly.

Capricorn and Virgo

Virgo and Capricorn will make a terrific couple. Just be careful not to become stuck in a suffocating rut. Both Virgo and Capricorn struggle to actively appreciate life. They should assist one another in this regard. Everything else went swimmingly.

Aquarius and Virgo

A Virgo-Aquarius relationship can work, but only with a lot of effort. Aquarius is overly demanding for Virgo: Virgo limits Aquarius' freedom. Aquarius is too unpredictable and irresponsible for Virgo, who needs organization and control. This will take a lot of perseverance and commitment.

Pisces and Virgo

To make a partnership between Virgo and Pisces succeed, Virgo must learn to manage its criticism. Pisces is so sensitive that it cannot stand being called out for errors. In this situation, Pisces will retreat into their fantasy world, and Virgo will be removed from the connection. The relationship might not have a healthy dynamic, so it may be preferable for them to part ways. These concerns can be addressed if they both choose to pursue the relationship. Virgo and Pisces are opposites on the health axis, yet they can find common ground in that they both want to do good.

LOVE AND PASSION

Some Virgos are reserved when it comes to physically showing their affection.

They prefer things to be pure and transparent, and they need to locate the appropriate environment to unwind. If their partners give them the trust they need, they will become open and honest lovers.

They are extremely devoted and expect the same in return. Virgos, who despise deception, try to be honest and direct with everyone.

They are not overly sentimental, and their cynicism often hinders them from forming deep and lasting bonds.

Some people get taken advantage of by people who aren't honest and want to take advantage of their kindness.

Virgos struggle to prioritize their own needs, and it is up to others to ensure that the Virgo's needs are not routinely ignored.

They make an effort to share their interests and live an active and enjoyable life as a couple.

MARRIAGE

They are generally supportive of marriage, but they must first fix their financial position before committing.

They should, on the other hand, temper their predisposition to dispute and criticize if they do not want to weaken their partner's morale and jeopardize the relationship.

In general, they strive like no one else to keep their marriage alive, but if they consider the disagreements are insurmountable, they will not hesitate to end it.

Virgo women, who are extremely adaptable, understand how to balance work and family duties. They want order and efficiency in their marriage, so when they do their married tasks, they do them with the best attitude possible.

Virgo males are also dedicated workers who value their roles as parents and husbands. Furthermore, they are not sexist and would never allow their spouse to perform more than their fair part.

CHAPTER TWO

VIRGO 2023 HOROSCOPE

Overview Virgo 2023

Jupiter, the planet of growth, begins the year in your 7th house of Aries and moves to your Eight house of Taurus in May 2023. As a result, your love/marriage will be blessed and happy during the first quarter. Then, with Jupiter's transit to the 8th house, problems arise. Saturn, the limiting planet, will remain in your 5th house of Aquarius until March when it will travel to your 6th house of Pisces. This will reduce your chances of luck, and you may have issues with children in the first quarter. Then Saturn may bring up health troubles and some form of spending, so be cautious.

This year, Uranus will be transiting your Taurus 9th house, ensuring general prosperity, while Neptune will be transiting your Pisces 7th house, impacting your love life. Pluto would be transiting Capricorn's 5th house before moving to Aquarius' 6th house in May/June 2023. These planetary transits would impact the Virgo's life during the year.

The year begins on a positive note for Virgo's love or marriage desires, owing to the influence of the planets of love, Venus and Mars. You would be lucky to keep your beloved or spouse in your net throughout the year. Your independence and sense of freedom may sometimes be tested, but keep going. Keep your cool and avoid situations that aren't suited for your relationship right now. Find out what works best for both of you. Your love life or marriage evolves slowly but steadily as the year progresses. Make plans for a brighter future with your partner. As the year comes to a close, your love or marriage will begin to bear fruit; you will marry if you haven't already, married people will most likely conceive, and if you already have a child, more are on the way.

Mars would begin the year 2023 by obstructing your career progress and development. You would run out of energy and enthusiasm to keep going. The first quarter might appear to have hit a brick wall, and the situation would become more favorable from a professional standpoint. Jupiter will bestow good fortune on you. If you own your firm, you can launch new endeavors. You would form stronger bonds with acquaintances, which would boost your professional status. You would benefit from partnerships and get more attention, respect, and status at work.

This year will be excellent for Virgos in terms of health. Jupiter's favorable aspects would increase your energy levels and make you more productive in your ideas and activities. Your overall health would be good, which would improve your professional performance. The positive influences on your ascendant house also portend excellent health and happiness throughout the year. However, some Virgos may suffer from weather-related ailments, but there will be no severe consequences. Those suffering from chronic illnesses should exercise caution during the middle of the year. That would be an unusual time for you to be especially careful. Regular medical help would help you stop any health problems before they worsen.

The year 2023 begins with Virgos in a fortunate economic situation. Jupiter's presence ensures a steady supply of cash for the people. Continue to work and explore all options for accumulating wealth. The planets assist you in taking any path that leads to financial security.

The planets will guide you to mature more gently in your domestic life this year. Saturn, however, will push you out of your comfort zone this year. During this time, you will be able to discover a lot more about yourself and your family members. Jupiter's transit in May might cause some uncertainty and misunderstandings in the family environment. Mars would provide the vitality you need to function successfully at home. Even if you deviate from your obligations, it will assist you in getting back on track.

The year 2023 would be pretty beneficial to Virgos' travel plans. Jupiter's relationship to your third house indicates that you will take several short trips this year. Those in the service industry would travel far and short distances extensively. You are also destined to go abroad this year due to the conjunction of Jupiter and Saturn in your 12th house of Leo.

All of your journeys have the potential to offer you benefits. The Moon's North node would aspect your 12th house during the latter part of the year, signifying an overseas trip.

In the life of Virgos, 2023 will be an excellent year for religious rituals. There would be far more devotion to your Gods than there has ever been before. This year, you will be able to make some sacrifices to your God. Going on pilgrimages or visiting holy locations will gain you merits. Jupiter's passage would urge you to give to charity and participate in social activities.

For the coming year, Virgos should avoid making hasty judgments. This year, use your energies to improve your relationships and money. Learn life lessons from the difficult challenges you are now facing. Do not be afraid to make amends or repairs when the occasion calls for it. Give your all to your relationships while being spiritually blessed. Saturn may hinder or confine your forward advance; do not lose heart; instead, be quiet and wait for the tide to change in your favor. And Jupiter would open fresh doors of opportunity this year, allowing you to master new talents.

January 2023

Horoscope

You live in an extremely comfortable environment. Capricorn's energies provide a sense of security. This has the effect of virtually boosting your self-esteem to new heights. You believe you can rely on your instincts.

This month, it will be your best guide. However, you will have to cope with Mars' dissonances in Gemini, which are creating havoc on your profession and prosperity. Your famous pragmatism will have a difficult time dealing with broken promises. Your sense of commitment increases tenfold around the 6th.

Take care not to drain yourself by catching up on other people's faults or taking on their obligations.

Love

The Capricorn planetary constellation drives your affections. It provides them with the stability you want.

This month looks peaceful because there is no extravagance around. But starting on the 28th, when Venus moves into Pisces, if you listen to its siren song, it can cause trouble.

Virgos in a healthy relationship, your relationship grows in a happy, helpful way that makes you want to plan for the future. But in the long run, your relationship can become tiresome. Listen to your gut when it gives you ideas that are out of the ordinary.

Virgo singles, A good star keeps an eye on the people you love. So, you get attention even when you don't do anything. At the end of the month, someone could be crazy about you and do everything they can to catch you. Believe in yourself.

Career

This is not a good month. On bad days, you feel like letting everything slip through your fingers, going on vacation, or quitting your job. Even though you may think you only have problems to solve, Virgo, you can look at things differently. What? 'Or' How? By seeing them as problems to you need and achieve your goals with unsettling ease.

Being organized will make it easier for you to get things done. Make a detailed list of the things you need to do each day. Strategize because it can make a big difference in how well you do. You tend to work too much, so plan your tasks wisely.

Surround yourself with good friends who think a lot like you. You will learn many life skills from them, and positive life experiences will help you slowly climb the ladder of success.

No one can tell you what will happen in your life, but you might lose if you let hard times get you down. Your career will require a lot of work, so learn if you have to and keep working to get better.

Finance

On the money front, everything is good for you to have fun. You don't have to spend a lot to be happy, and your costs aren't too high to get you in trouble.

The stars say that this month will be good for your money, and there are signs that investments or stock trading will make you a lot of money. So, you can take some calculated risks with your money this month. Relationships with your bosses or coworkers are also likely to get better without any trouble, to the point where big gains are almost certain.

The climate would be good for new investments or business ideas. You have great ideas for running a business or investing money. Find time to tell the people you trust about these things. You will get good advice on planning and carrying out your ideas.

Health

Maintaining a healthy lifestyle is made easier this month by the constellations that are aligned in your favor. Those with a propensity to stomach and digestive issues would be greatly alleviated. Coughs, colds, and asthma, all common disorders of the chest, will be eliminated.

You'll recuperate more quickly when you have someone to look after you. It's time to look for people who can physically and morally help you. As we get older, our bodies deteriorate and require emotional support.

Understandably, you'd want to keep an eye on your oral health because it may cause you pain, but with the proper dental care, you won't have to worry. It's possible that you're easily agitated and have a little disturbed state of mind. Keeping your mind and body in a state of calm and balance won't take much work and will help you stay in.

Travel

There isn't much chance of making money from travel this month, since the stars don't look good on this front. Most of the time this month, you would travel alone, mostly by car or train, with some air travel thrown in.

Also, you might work or travel abroad. But it is almost certain that these efforts would not bring the profits, pleasure, and satisfaction that were hoped for. The best direction would be to go East.

Insight from the stars

You are no longer required to demonstrate your sincerity. Remember, though, that some people are more relaxed than you. It would be a shame if your popularity dwindled. This month, you will have to develop new ways to use your skills, talents, and abilities.

February 2023

Horoscope

The dissonances emanating from Pisces and Gemini disrupt your peace this month. These energies throw you off balance and use all means possible to disrupt your well-organized existence. At first sight, you may believe that the sky and stars intend to cause havoc. If you examine closely, you will notice that some minor modifications will do you a world of good.

You must take a step back before rejecting a confession of love or making a decision to succeed at this little feat. This may involve some work on your part, but it will spare you from having regrets later on. Be extremely cautious around the 20th since the new moon occurs in Pisces.

Love

Pisces' energies are trying to get you to make a commitment. In return, this possibility is likely to make you lose control. Instead of getting defensive, take a deep breath and think. This will help you find a solution that works for both of you.

Virgos, your partner is the one who drives your relationship forward. This approach suggests that there will be some emotional trouble. If you want to get along with your partner, respond to one of their requests.

Virgo singles, Your desire to meet someone and have a beautiful love story is confirmed. But that's no reason to start something that won't work out for you in the long run. Keep time for yourself to keep this from happening.

Career

Although it is not easy, great things are coming this month. Your task appears less complex, but you approach it with greater optimism. However, you will most likely feel the time is too long and wish for a change. Unfortunately, what is provided falls short of your expectations. If you want to see things improve in this industry, Virgo, focus on the positives rather than the flaws.

You would have good prospects for career advancement if your circumstances were suitable because you will put in the effort and succeed in achieving your goals. There is a good possibility that this will open up a whole new world of opportunities for you, leading to a much better career or a shift in business operations. It's all for the better.

You should also anticipate significant travel, which will be really useful. The most advantageous direction would be east. This phase will also be marked by a daring attitude in your professional pursuits. This would result in improved efficiency and leadership skills.

Finance

On the financial front, if a purchase necessitates hefty financing, you're in luck. But that is no excuse for abusing it. Promise?

However, the stars predict that the course of events will not favor your financial progress this month. True, there are obvious signs that your investments may result in significant losses. As a result, it would be prudent to avoid all forms of gambling.

There are also indicators that any disagreement or litigation you may be involved in will probably be resolved against you, resulting in significant losses. As a result, you must work hard to ensure that any such choice is postponed until a later and more suitable time. Relationships with superiors, business partners, or workers are also likely to deteriorate; avoid such a scenario, or you may incur significant losses.

Health

The augury of stars facing you this month has a lot of good news for your health. Any tendency to sudden acute diseases, such as fever or inflammations, would get significant alleviation, even if only for a short time. Such an issue would most likely not worry you at all. Back pain would be alleviated in the same way.

Attempt to be productive without jeopardizing your health. The best thing you can do is start with what you consume. Prepare a menu of all the foods you enjoy and make healthier versions.

However, there are reasons to be concerned about the likelihood of an eye infection. This may irritate you temporarily, but it is preventable with adequate preventative measures such as cleanliness and the use of appropriate preventive medicine. Overall, a month is fairly promising for your health.

Travel

As far as making money from travel is concerned, the horoscope from the stars doesn't say anything particularly good. This month, you would travel alone mostly by car and train, with some flights.

An international trip is also a possibility. There's a good chance that these efforts won't bring the profits or pleasures hoped for. This is a pretty dark picture, but unfortunately, it's true. A lot of your travel may not be necessary, and you could probably do fine without it. The most favorable direction is East.

Insight from the stars

Even if it's tempting, don't go overboard. Find the best compromise for each situation so everyone can get what they want. Approach life with confidence. Don't let anyone make decisions for you. You have everything you need to make the right choices in your life.

March 2023

Horoscope

This month, you'll have to deal with the dissonances caused by Gemini and Pisces. These energies interrupt both your plans and your peace. They give you the impression that you are being bombarded by occurrences. You get the sensation that your spouse, boss, and others do not comprehend your point of view.

You've lost command of the situation. These occurrences are increased and verified around the 7th when the full moon forms in your sign. Instead of fighting in all directions, look at things from a new perspective. Be open to new possibilities. This possibility is provided by Uranus and Venus in Taurus. Certainly surprising, but if you desire serenity, it is important to give it some thought.

Love

Even though you want to help, it's hard unless you agree to look at things differently. You feel pressure from the forces in Pisces, and Venus in Taurus winks at you. Despite what you think, you have a choice this month and can make a choice.

Still, people are angry about commitment. Your partner criticizes you all the time. When Venus is in Taurus and Mars is in Cancer, you can make a distraction. Show off all your good qualities. It will make your partner feel calm and safe.

Virgo singles, From the 17th, Venus in Taurus plays Cupid. From the 26th, Mars in Cancer urges you to take action. Your loves could match your aspirations if you listen to your gut and not your mind.

Career

Saturn might be blamed for making you feel as if your horizon is obstructed. Aside from demoralizing you, it accentuates the obstacles that Mars in Gemini sends your way. Virgo admits that this month hasn't been all that bright. You can, however, have a unique perspective on it. Is there any other way? By putting a stop to the pursuit of excellence. Doing this will save a great deal of time and improve the quality of your life.

This is a great month to take your career to the next level. Those drawn to the arts and those who practice the fine arts should expect a period of creative fulfilment. With your efforts, you may build a name for yourself in the future.

There would also be a lot of travel involved, which would be quite helpful. The south would be the best route to travel. Aside from travel, you may have to relocate your operation's location, whether it's for work or pleasure. Take your time and think things over thoroughly before making any changes. Otherwise, you might undo all of your hard work.

Finance

A sizable amount of overdue money might fill your piggy bank and give you peace of mind. The stars are aligned in your favor regarding your financial situation this month. As you succeed in your commercial endeavors and investments, you will have a stable source of income. The problem is that excessive expenditure might lead to bankruptcy. Save money by spending a little.

You'll be able to put your money to work for you this month. This month, you have a terrific opportunity to make money by investing in stocks or franchising. You'd likely make a tidy profit from your investments and company ventures.

Health

This month, you have a good set of circumstances for your health. Chronic diseases like rheumatism, gout, and problems with the digestive system like flatulence and too much wind would get a lot better. This should not, however, be taken as a pass to stop being careful.

There are reasons to be a little worried about the state of your teeth. Take care of your teeth and Try to improve your health overall. Make an effort to break bad habits and plan outdoor activities that you can do every day. Make it a habit to make time for these activities, even if you have a busy schedule.

You have a good month ahead, during which you won't have to deal with serious health risks.

Travel

Not a good month to go on a trip because the stars don't seem particularly favorable in this regard, especially if you want to make a lot of money from it. Writers, poets, and others like them may have a financially and creatively unproductive travel period.

You would usually travel alone, mostly by car or train, with a fair amount of flying. A trip overseas is not impossible. But it's almost certain that these efforts won't even come close to reaching a fraction of the goals. The best way to go is to the South.

Insight from the stars

Quit trying to meet everyone else's needs! Think about yourself instead. Do yourself a favor, and don't worry if it bothers people who mean well. Take advantage of the chances that keep knocking on your door to move up in your career.

April 2023

Horoscope

With Saturn in your sign, you'll have to deal with its demands and dreams. Taurus and Cancer energies assist you to succeed in this tiny miracle. They encourage you to try out new solutions to your behavior and inspire you to use your abilities and follow your intuition.

This month, events and circumstances inspire you to put the virtues of letting go to the test since difficulties grow with Venus in Gemini between the 12th and 30th. Taking a step back will allow you to have a more hopeful outlook on the future. This can also help you understand that you have a lot more options than you believe.

Love

Saturn makes you feel more responsible, but it can also get you and the people you love into a lot of trouble. To avoid this, pay attention to what Venus and Mercury in Taurus tell you to do. Don't be as shy as you usually are. Accept that you deserve to enjoy life a little bit more.

Virgos in a relationship: The air between you two is a little cold. Mercury helps you figure out why you're here this month. Also, it gives you ideas that you should use if you want to start a conversation.

Single Virgos, up until the 11th, your love looks good. Then the atmosphere becomes colder. Instead of jumping from one idea to the next, be more spontaneous if you want to catch up. Don't try to change the people you love. Instead, accept them as they are.

Career

Investment and trust are two of the most important factors for a person's success. Virgo, this is your chance to show the world what you're made of. Removing these impediments will help you go forward. Because, even though you may believe you don't have enough time to get everything done, you do.

This month has been a good one regarding your career future. Fine artists and others of their type would enjoy themselves much. With your efforts, you may build a name for yourself in the future. There are hints that you are prone to working hard and achieving your goals on time. And you will succeed in this as well.

Your location may change even if you're running a business or providing a service. Change should only be made after much thought and consideration. Additionally, there would be significant travel, which would be highly advantageous in the long run.

Finance

Although your piggy bank is full, you may have to cut some corners financially to maintain your standard of living. The end of the month is approaching, and while it's not something you want to do, you may be forced to utilize your resources to catch up.

Because of the unfavorable constellations in your chart, your financial situation isn't looking well this month. You stand to suffer significant losses as a result of speculation. The lesson is clear: avoid all forms of gambling at all costs.

In addition, it is possible that your relationship with your superiors may deteriorate to the point where losses are a real possibility. Prevent this from happening by acting quickly to correct the situation. Due to the sluggish economy, investing or establishing

new initiatives will be difficult. To put it another way,
these plans should be put on hold for the time being.

Health

In the constellations that are aligned to face you this
month, you have plenty of reasons to be optimistic
about your health. The signs warn you not to push
yourself too much. This should be avoided at all costs
if you want to keep things running normally and not
stress the system.

Make it easier on yourself by making a new
schedule of activities. Maintaining good oral health is
important, and you should take all the necessary
precautions to ensure that you do. From a health
perspective, you have fairly positive month.

Travel

This month, your chances of making money from
travel aren't very good because the stars aren't in your
favor on this score. This month, you would probably
travel alone by train, car, and air.

Also, a trip abroad is not impossible. But one thing
is certain: these trips would not accomplish even a
fraction of the objectives. The majority of this travel

would be unrelated to your business or job. The best direction would be to go West.

Insights from the stars

Your sense of order and method is indisputable? Just the opposite. Still, try not to control everything. Let things happen naturally. You will have to find a way to balance your work and your personal life. You've been ignoring your loved ones for a while and need to start paying more attention to them.

May 2023

Horoscope

Saturn keeps pushing you back into your comfort zones while also trying to open your eyes to a new way of seeing the world. As a consequence, you may feel terrific at times and depressed at others. Support from Taurus and Cancer is benevolent yet practical and helps you keep going and helps you locate the materials needed to satisfy Saturn's requirements. They provide you with the security you need to avoid making poor choices. However, a little divine guidance wouldn't hurt!

May 17th marks the arrival of Jupiter, the promising star and evolutionary force, in Taurus. It opens up new opportunities that have been wanted for a while.

Love

Saturnian forces direct your attention here. As a result, you have an austere, gloomy, and often critical view of the situation. Fortunately, friendly planetary energies provide a distraction! They force you to encounter people who can influence your opinion.

Virgos in a relationship, the mood is always a little heavy, but don't worry, everything is OK! You have everything you need to make things go more smoothly. Don't be afraid to utilize it; your other half will thank you.

Virgo singles, the stars recommend you have a charming and delicate meeting. Allow things to happen without interrogating them. If you want to do something, do it! Go for it while you're feeling it!

Career

You do a good job of insuring in your industry. It's OK to ask for help, but don't be afraid to ask for it! Jupiter is in Taurus at the time of its arrival. As Virgos, this is the time to pay attention to what's going on in the world. Think about it if someone offers you a great deal. And don't think you can't do it because you can.

This is a month in which you have little chance of moving up in your profession, and if you're not cautious, you may end up lower on the ladder than you started. You may be tempted to break the law for short-term gains. In the event that this is permitted to happen, the repercussions will be catastrophic. To avoid falling

prey to such temptations, you must make a clear
commitment to yourself.

There is also a chance that you will have severe
disagreements with your superiors. This is something
else you should work hard to avoid. As a result of your
unease, you're more likely to switch jobs or work with
other colleagues. Only make alterations after thorough
consideration. Only make changes after careful
thought.

Finance

When it comes to money and modest presents, they
can help ease tensions, but you don't need to go over
your budget. Don't overspend, but do it generously.

This month's horoscope isn't in your favor
regarding your financial situation. You will lose
money when you trade and invest. This means that you
should avoid any investments.

In addition, there are reasons to believe that your
relationships with your superiors will suffer due to
your tendency to dispute, which might result in
significant financial losses. You have the power to
prevent this if you work hard enough. To avoid such a
situation, you should take the necessary precautions in
advance. If you were planning on making any

investments or starting any new ventures this month, you'd be better off waiting.

Health

This month, the stars don't have any good news for your health. So, you need to be more cautious and watchful. Those who are more likely to get piles should be very careful about what they eat and how they are treated. Carelessness would only make things worse.

Pay attention to your health and get help for the difficult disease you are dealing with. Even if you have to wait to see a doctor or if you get the wrong diagnosis, you will still get the proper treatment you need. Be humble and use the available medical options.

Any tendency to get colds or have a lot of mucus come out may worsen. Again, this could need quick attention and corrective actions to make things right. Stones and a tendency to get fistula would also need more attention, as would your teeth. Take care of your teeth as this might cause you problems as well.

Travel

A month in which you might lose a lot of money while travelling because the stars aren't very favorable. During your travels, you might get hurt or have some other kind of physical problem. Exercise care and minimize risks.

You would travel alone mostly by car and train, but you would also take a fair amount of flights. A journey overseas is also not out of the question. These stays could end up being utterly useless in every way. Since only some of them would be done for business purposes, they wouldn't make the expected money. The rest wouldn't make you happy. North is the best direction to go.

Insight from the stars

Take a step back when things start to make sense. This will help you understand what they are saying and what you need to do to calm down. Don't miss out on anything that could help your career. Now is the time to reach significant goals in your life.

June 2023

Horoscope

Gains, ties, or a way of life become outmoded due to Saturn's dissonances. Despite your excellent intentions, they will not be able to deliver you much more. Jupiter's fortunate presence in Taurus provides you with the opportunity to make changes.

The lucky star urges you to broaden your sphere of activity through events and situations, allowing you to meet individuals who are unlike you. He encourages you to put your talents and skills to good use.

Unfortunately, an opportunity is sometimes accompanied by a problem that must be solved, so you must overcome your reservations. If you want to capitalize on the opportunities that may occur, you must dare to talk about yourself and your abilities. Be a little opportunistic, and know that no one will judge you for it.

Love

You start to doubt your ability to seduce because of things that happen or how other people act. You don't feel like you have anything in common with people you think are more successful. You are probably thinking about something. Luckily, the light starts to come on the 22nd.

If you're in a relationship, it might not be clear, but your relationship could change. You can stop being so bored, which is bad for your morale if you want to. Let go to make this little trick work.

Virgo singles, the stars are being funny this month and putting you in touch with good people. Instead of thinking about yourself all the time, enjoy life and everything it offers.

Career

The little boost that was hoped for is coming, but it won't be enough. Do you want things to change, Virgo? So, instead of focusing on what's wrong, look at everything you do well and do even better! At first, this may seem impossible, but if you give yourself time, you'll get there so easily that it will shock you. You will get the satisfaction you want if you do this.

As far as your professional future goes, the horoscope doesn't tell you anything particularly good. There is a good chance you will have a big disagreement with your bosses or business partner. This shouldn't be allowed to happen, and you should try to stop it from happening.

You might also be filled with a feeling of insecurity that would affect almost everything you do at work. You could try to even things out by switching jobs quickly or making changes to how your business works. This would be a terrible way for things to be. Any change should be made only after a lot of careful thought. There would also be a lot of travel, but this wouldn't lead to much either.

Finance

When it comes to money, you can live a normal life, but the stars put you on a budget when it comes to fancy things. A good month for your finances. You can look forward to getting a lot of money quickly, and you would also be better off if you invested. There is also a good chance that an old friend will do you a favor that could be very helpful financially.

Also, this month you'll learn how to deal with your bosses, which will make the relationship very good for you. This could be a big advantage. Lastly, being friends with many intelligent, spiritually-minded people with gifts would help you in both material and spiritual ways.

Health

This month, the stars are favoring your well-being, and you should enjoy a period of good health. Sudden acute illnesses like fevers and inflammation would be significantly reduced. You would be completely unaffected by them.

People with any kind of dental issue will also benefit from this blessing. In fact, any issue with your dentures should be taken carefully and has a strong probability of being resolved. This is a good time for your health, and those currently in good condition may anticipate continuing in good shape.

Travel

Since the stars aren't in a good place this month, you shouldn't expect to get what you want out of travel, nor will you have as much fun as you thought. If you want to go on a pilgrimage to a holy place, the trip might have to be put off, or you might run into problems along the way.

Most of the time, you travel alone by train or car, with some flights thrown in. Even a trip abroad is not impossible. Still, none of these efforts would get anywhere. The best way to go is to the East.

Insight from the stars

If you want things to progress, you must be brave
and agree to meet new people. Talk about yourself,
your accomplishments, and your goals. Your career
will go well, and you will work with people who are
goal-oriented and focused.

July 2023

Horoscope

Even though Jupiter is the "star of evolution" and gives you chances to do more, Saturn and Neptune are bad news. They make you doubt yourself, which stops you from moving forward. You find it hard to see the good things about the opportunities that come your way. They make you feel bad about yourself, which makes you want to be alone, although Mercury makes it easy to see clearly until the 11th. The advice you get from your relationships is wise and insightful.

Mars moves into your sign on the 11th, which makes you more likely to take charge. It forces you to overcome your fears and take what's on offer. You're bursting at the seams this month, but you can change how things go if you want to.

Love

This month, you have serious doubts about your ability to attract a partner. You can stop this torturous process if you want to. How? Realizing that you have good qualities and everything you need to please someone who wants a real relationship based on intelligence.

If you're a Virgo in a relationship, Saturn will slow things down and cause trouble. Even though Mercury brings back the conversations, there is a lot of silence from the 11th to the 28th. Your options are limited but don't worry, providence will make things right again.

The stars tell you to stay put if you're a single Virgo. Another person sets you up with someone interested in you because of your qualities. Don't pay attention to what's wrong. Take the right path in life.

Career

You may think that things are getting worse as the days go by. It's easy to believe that things and people deliberately try to aggravate you during the worst days. In reality, Virgo, that's not what's going on here. You'll be pushed to new heights by these conditions and these individuals! So, rely on your intuition, abilities, and experience to make the best decisions for you. You'll be able to achieve great things if you do this!

This month, your astrological chart shows just a few promising omens for professional growth. You'd likely put in a lot of effort, but you wouldn't be able to achieve your goals. Disputes with your superiors are also a probable possibility.

Because of the potentially devastating outcomes, this must be avoided at all costs. Try to anticipate and work around any challenging areas that may arise. There would also be a lot of travel, which would, unfortunately, provide nothing in the way of rewards, but a short trip to the South may yield a little percentage for you.

Finance

The worry of running out of money causes you to be extremely frugal. But don't deprive yourself of everything!

If things go smoothly for you this month, there is a strong chance that your financial situation will be stable for the foreseeable future. You might be able to expect to get a lot of unexpected benefits and money from your investments.

If you're a manager, you'll have a system for managing your subordinates or employees that maximizes your return on investment. This would be a huge advantage for you and could even lead to massive profits. Another possibility is that an old buddy may do you a favor or provide you with a service that will be highly helpful.

Health

It's not a good month for your health, as Lady Fortune isn't being cooperative this month and is withholding her blessings. Predispositions to chronic conditions like rheumatism and digestive abnormalities such as gas and extra wind in the digestive system would be more bothersome than usual. As with any type of dental issue, more attention and care are required.

In addition, you may be bothered by a predisposition to anxiety. You should take extra precautions to protect your health in the next few months, as the future seems bleak.

Travel

A month in which the chances of profiting from travel look slim, as the stars are not in a good mood. You would most likely travel alone by rail and road, with some air travel thrown in for good measure. International travel is also not out of the question.

All of these trips might be related to work and other things in equal measure. But no matter why you're traveling, it's almost certain that you won't reach even a fraction of your goals. As a result, it's a good idea to go over your travel plans ahead of time to see if they'll get you anywhere. The best direction to go would be South.

Insight from the stars

Despite what you think, you have everything you need to change how things are going. How? By making the most of the opportunities that come your way. If you don't live healthily, it could hurt your health.

August 2023

Horoscope

Saturn has been telling you for a while that your relationships won't help you much. Your conversations have become less interesting. With people you've known for years, a distance grows. Time makes bonds weaken. In exchange, Uranus and Jupiter provide opportunities to meet new people. They want you to grow up in a different universe of relationships, but one that fits you from now on. If you agree, you can get out of this boring situation this month.

Mars in your sign gives you the courage and daring to take what's offered to you, which helps you do this little trick. Mercury, which is also in Virgo, makes you more understanding, enabling you to make social, friendly, and other connections.

Love

Even though your friends or dates show you the opposite, you're starting to doubt your ability to seduce.

Try to be less hard on yourself and look on the bright side of things.

Virgos in a relationship, the mood is dark, but you have the power to change it. At the end of the month, Mars, Mercury, and the sun give you the energy and ideas you need to rebuild your relationship.

Single Virgos If you stay stuck in romantic plans from the past, you will be bored. On the other hand, if you don't question the unexpected and just go with it, you give yourself the best chance of meeting someone amazing.

Career

Now is an excellent time to reflect on your goals. Look over the proposed changes while you're at it, too. Consider them thoroughly and without bias. Never, ever, ever assume it's not for you. An inexplicable transformation has begun in Virgo! Even if you think it's bad news, it's actually quite good for your well-being. Why? for the simple reason that it will allow you to see things in a new light.

An unfavorable month for advancing one's career, as well as a time when one should exercise extra caution. There's a good chance that you and your superiors will have some major disagreements. Ideally, you should avoid this at all costs. Keep your cool and steer clear of problem situations by remaining calm and patient this month.

You may be tempted to break the law to make a fast buck. If you don't want to end up in the abyss, you'll need to rein in these impulses.

Finance

When it comes to money, you can keep your focus on the important things if you save. You think futility is a gimmick. Your financial situation has suddenly improved!

This is a month in which you have the potential to make a significant amount of money if you behave wisely.

You'll have a better shot at financial advancement. Leaving your former job or profession might lead to a rich new opportunity. Despite the fact that money isn't your primary goal, your hunt for a superior firm or business opportunity will result in unanticipated financial gains. It will help you and your family save a lot of money.

You may make a lot of money by investing. As a result, you must take advantage of any opportunity. Stock trading, gambling, and creating new ventures would all thrive in this environment.

Health

This month's horoscopes do not bode well for your health. A tendency to be nervous could be a problem, and any kind of tooth trouble is likely to need more care and attention. This should be taken seriously. There are more reasons to think that you may be in a state of general weakness and nervous problems due to overwork and exhaustion.

You can avoid this by redrawing your schedule and then sticking to it. This would help you a lot and solve a lot of your problems. Clearly, the time ahead of you isn't very good, so you should be very careful and watchful.

Travel

There's nothing particularly fortunate about what the stars say about what you'll gain from travelling. This month, you would travel almost equally for work, business, and other reasons.

You would probably travel alone most of the time, mostly by road and train. A trip abroad also can't be ruled out. No matter why or how you travel, it's almost certain that you won't get even a fraction of what you planned to get out of it—thinking carefully about your travel plans before you make them would be wise. West would be the best direction.

Insights from the stars

You begin to notice that a new relationship is creeping into your life. You won't have to worry about being criticized as long as you maintain your composure. Give back to the community by getting involved in charitable endeavors that benefit those less fortunate.

September 2023

Horoscope

Contrary to popular belief, you have everything you need to start living a more peaceful and enjoyable life.

As a result of the influence of Taurus and Virgo, your growth and success are more possible. Mercury makes you more intelligent. As a result, you have a more precise understanding of what you mean. It encourages you to recognize and make use of your natural talents. It's possible to alter the path of events if you agree with this. How? By Taking advantage of the possibilities that will present themselves and not wasting time on self-reflection! If you're worried about everything working smoothly, don't be! Things are going to go smoothly and at a reasonable pace.

Love

Bad memories start to bubble up. Suddenly, you're feeling down! You don't get better. Your relationship will be back on a smooth path soon, free of the hurts and disappointments of the past. Try to smile again and trust yourself until then.

If you're a Virgo in a relationship, you lose your passion and grow apart. Sadness is in the air. Your relationship needs to get back on track as soon as possible. The fights can get heated this month, but they can also bring your relationship back to life.

Virgo singles, situations make you feel like you might stay single forever. Don't worry, this is not the case. This month, agree to meet someone who isn't like the people you usually date.

Career

This month, the stars allow you plenty of time to contemplate making a business proposal. Taking advantage of this window of opportunity is an excellent idea. This will enable you to make a decision free of outside influence. The 16th is a good day to clean up your documents or computer if you suddenly decide to do so.

There isn't much hope for your professional future in the current month's astrological configuration. Serious disagreements with your superiors are very likely. This would be a disaster waiting to happen. That's why avoiding a situation like this is so important.

There's also the possibility that an unnecessary sense of insecurity plagues you. Resolving this issue may require you to look for new employment or change how you do business. A terrible situation to find yourself in. Take your time and think things out before making any adjustments.

Finance

Keeping your financial life balanced relies on your capacity to make rational decisions about your spending and saving. And if your loved ones come to you and beg for your help, don't be unreasonable in your response.

According to the astrological forecast, it will not be a good month for your finances. There's a good chance your relationships with your superiors will deteriorate to the point where you'll be forced to take a hit financially. If you want to avoid such a scenario, you need to plan ahead to ensure you're prepared.

There would be a lack of possibilities, and you would have difficulty reaching your goals. Additionally, you risk being too obsessed with producing money you can't account for. This will have a negative impact on your current circumstances. Correct the situation. This includes avoiding investments and gambling.

Health

It will not be a great month for your health since the stars aren't feeling generous. For susceptible people, having cold hands and feet would be a nightmare. Any tendency to anxiety would just become worse. There's a strong chance that a skilled yoga teacher and regular practice can help you overcome this problem.

There's a greater chance of having an issue with your teeth. This implies that your tooth health will receive further attention. As a result, your health will require more attention and care in the weeks ahead.

Travel

This is a month in which it may be hard to make money from travelling since the prophesy from the stars is not favorable on this front. A pilgrimage to a holy place would have to be postponed or become bogged down in problems.

Anyone hoping to further their education by going to college or training programs in another country or continent may face some unexpectedly challenging obstacles. You'd largely use the road and train to go about on your own, with some flights thrown in. The possibility of an overseas trip is not ruled out. A trip abroad is also not out of the question. On the other hand, these stays would be a total waste of time. North is the best direction to go.

Insight from the stars

You can alter the path of events. It's better to meet people who live in a different reality than yours to stop repeating your own views and ideas to yourself endlessly. With better lines of communication, your romantic life will flourish.

October 2023

Horoscope

Venus takes control on the 10th, and Mercury leaves on the 5th. Mars enters Scorpio on the 13th. Mercury and the Sun will join him at the end of the month. It's a great time to make changes because Saturn is retrograde and Jupiter is slowing down. Because of the planets in Scorpio, you're in an excellent place to move forward. Saturn in Pisces is a symbol of obstacles that you can conquer.

The people you surround yourself with are the most important part of your support system. There are several ways in which it aids you in recognizing and capitalizing on your worth. If you don't know what to think about a possible opportunity or proposal this month, ask people you trust what they think.

Love

After the 10th, you start to feel better. Venus makes it easier to deal with Saturn. She tells you to stop thinking about the past and focus on yourself. This month, you should change your look and say yes to your friends' offers.

Virgos who are dating, even though the mood is sad, you get a second wind. Mars and Venus want you to take charge of the situation to get your relationship moving again. This month, stop talking and start doing something.

Virgo singles, Don't even think about getting married at any costs! Think about yourself and what's happening now. Also, instead of turning down the invitations, accept them. You will meet new people if you do this.

Career

You are on the verge of fulfilling your request for growth or change. You must decide for this tiny miracle to occur. When it comes to work, you're a Virgo who tends to overthink everything. This is a certain way to end yourself right back where you started. If that's not what you're looking for, talk to someone you can rely on. When you hear what they say, you'll be surprised. The more you listen to them, the more you'll be happy.

According to the stars, this is not a great month for your career future. If you're feeling good about yourself, you could consider changing jobs or making a significant adjustment to your business or service. Because of this, there is a good chance that you will disagree with your bosses or those above you.

There would also be a lot of hard effort, which would fail to achieve the intended outcomes and leave you terribly disappointed. Always maintain some kind of consistency and avoid acting erratically.

Finance

You spend a lot of money because you are in love with someone. So, if you don't want to become broke, you might want to slow down.

According to the stars' interpretation, this month's horoscope does not portend well for your financial well-being. As a result of your tendency to engage in conflict with your superiors, you might suffer a significant setback in your career. To avoid this, you should take whatever precautions you can think of to prevent it.

Some of you would almost certainly suffer losses due to your speculative activities. Gambling should thus be avoided in general. The climate would likewise be unsuitable for making investments or establishing new enterprises. Such ideas should be put on hold for the time being.

Health

This month's star alignment does not provide much hope for better health on your part. People prone to sudden acute illness may be bothered by short-lived bouts of illness. These should be dealt with as soon as possible.

Dental care should be given significantly more importance and all possible measures implemented to preserve healthy teeth and gums. In contrast to other months, this one calls for a higher level of focus than usual.

There may be issues with the mind, such as anxiety and other mental health issues. Calmness and balance must be maintained, with a special effort to stay upbeat and pleasant. Maintaining a healthy diet, regular exercise, and adequate sleep are all necessary for good health. Any excess can lead to an unbalanced existence.

Avoid exhaustion by not overworking. Do not overindulge in eating since this will lead to weight gain. Limiting your intake of alcohol might lead to a higher risk of drunkenness, so be careful. By keeping things in moderation, you'll be able to ensure that your body is in good shape.

Travel

This isn't a good month to travel because the stars aren't aligned in a way that makes it easy to get where you want to go. There is a chance that you will get hurt or have some other kind of physical problem while you are travelling. So, you should be careful and take the fewest possible risks.

Most of the time, you would travel by rail or road, but you would also fly a fair amount. Some of your trips might be related to your job or business. A good number of them wouldn't be so similar. It's pretty clear that none of these would be beneficial. A trip abroad is also not impossible. The best way to go is to the east.

Insight from the stars

Let go of the past's influence this month and have faith in your own abilities. You may count on your closest friends to introduce you to new people. Be prepared for significant changes in your life, and be ready to welcome them all.

November 2023

Horoscope

Jupiter in Taurus opens doors for you. As for the planets in Scorpio, they give you the power to get what you want. You may wonder what the problem is in this environment, which is very good for your growth.

Mercury, the Sun, and Mars are all in the sign of Sagittarius, which creates many different problems. But if you want to, you can get past them. Stop being content with the little you have if you want this little miracle to work. Dare to ask for more because you should. For once, try to make friends. And if you're worried about what will happen, don't be. With the energies that flow through Scorpio, you don't have to worry about going too far.

Love

If you don't let go of the past, the people you love will have a hard time. You will keep making mistakes, and you won't get anywhere. On the other hand, things will be a lot better if you can get away from it. You will meet people who are charming and can decide what to do.

For Virgos in a relationship, the planets in Scorpio will help you take charge. Unfortunately, disagreements can get in the way of this happiness. Your relationship isn't easy this month, but don't worry, it's not in danger.

This month, Virgo singles won't fall in love at first sight, but they will find a great match with someone they already know. Stop asking yourself questions if you want this small wonder to come true. Just live in the moment.

Career

You're in a better position than you've ever been. If you accept a given proposal, you might alter your course of action. However, this may only be achieved if you're willing to take on various tasks. Focus on the positive aspects of a shift instead of the negative ones. Make an effort to see the positive side of things for once. You'll be able to break free of this routine by doing so.

There isn't a lot of good news for your job chances this month, thanks to the constellation of stars. A sense of uneasiness about your job might keep you up at night. You'd have to rethink everything you do in connection with your company or work.

Even if you put in a lot of time and effort, your goals may still elude you. As a result, you'd either look for a new career or significantly adjust your business operations. However, you would still be unhappy with all of this. An even more serious confrontation is possible with your bosses. This should be avoided at all costs. Be proactive and try to predict and solve problems before they happen so you can avoid them.

Finance

Due to a favorable alignment of the stars, you should have a good month in terms of earning potential this month. Artists of all types are set to have a particularly fruitful month in terms of creative production and financial success in the coming weeks.

The tides are turning in your favor, and you may be in line for a windfall of unexpected riches. Profits might also be made through investments. Depending on your luck, you could even receive some cash assistance from one of your female friends!

Health

This month, a good set of events would make you feel good about your health. People prone to chronic diseases like rheumatism and digestive problems like flatulence and too much gas would feel a lot better. This means you wouldn't have to worry about these problems if you took normal precautions.

But there are reasons to be careful about throat pain that doesn't go away. This should be carefully looked into to see if there are any complications, and then it should be treated with care. If you don't do this, you could mess up a good health situation. Besides this, you don't have any serious reasons to worry.

Travel

It might be hard to make money from travel this month since the stars don't look good on this front. Musicians, painters, dancers, and other artists may not get as much out of their trips as they usually do. In fact, this could be a setback for some of them.

Most of the time, you would travel by rail or road, with a fair amount of air travel. A trip abroad is also not out of the question. Most of this would be related to your business or job, but these efforts wouldn't get you where you want to go. The best way to go is toward the East.

Insights from the stars

Don't suffer Saturn's effects; instead, use them to your advantage. This month, stay away from people who don't suit you and get closer to those who do. Things in your life seem to be going in the right direction. You will have more happiness and peace than ever before.

December 2023

Horoscope

You feel calm when Taurus, Capricorn, and Scorpio send out their energies. You feel like you're growing up in a world that fits and gets you. Your relationships with the people you care about are built on strong, honest bonds. You think you are going in the right direction, and you are. So, you have to be practical to take advantage of the opportunities that come your way.

Unfortunately, Sagittarius's dissonances and Saturn's position in Pisces create risks and tensions. If you have trouble, your progress will be slowed down. On the other hand, nothing can stop you if you know what they mean. This month, your growth will depend on how well you can act despite problems.

Love

When Venus is in Scorpio, your relationships are stable and pleasant. You feel like you're surrounded by people who really care about you. Unfortunately, tensions from the outside world get in the way of these joys. Use it to make decisions that will set you free instead of making you stuck.

Even though you and your partner are getting along better, tensions from the outside are trying to cause trouble. You have a choice this month. You can relax and talk to them or ignore them until they get bored.

Venus helps Virgo singles find love by bringing them together with someone they already know. If you want this new happiness to grow calmly, don't tell anyone about it. On the other hand, you have to be determined if you want to show it in broad daylight.

Career

You keep doing your best this month, and it works out well for you. You might feel like you're on the right end of the rope! Unfortunately, the dissonances that come from Pisces and Sagittarius can hit you hard and hold you back. Virgo, if you stop at the first problem, you won't get very far. On the other hand, you get around it with the intelligence that defines you. You will do wonders.

According to the stars, there is a lot of good news about your career this month. Your career will also undergo sudden changes, but most of them will be good. You might get a raise or a new job or find other opportunities.

But you'll probably be busier because you'll have to do more tasks and have more responsibilities at work. You are usually a workaholic, but your plate will be too full this month, and you may feel stressed and tired. But don't worry, your coworkers or business partners will come to your aid.

Don't worry about asking for help. Teamwork is the key to getting through challenging situations at work. Give the tasks to the other people on the team.

Finance

Spending money on frivolous items is no longer an option. First things first. As a result, your financial account will benefit greatly.

As you invest in real estate this month, you may expect a steady flow of income. At the same time, you have a solid financial foundation to meet your obligations when they come due. A lot of physical and mental effort may be needed this month to manage your finances properly. It's going to be difficult, but it's going to be worth it.

However, you still need to exercise caution. It is essential to save your money for financial security. You may even be able to help people in need by sharing your blessings. If this is a good month, you might want to invest in making passive income.

Health

This month, the alignment of the stars is in your favor and is beneficial to your health. Those with an acute chest or lungs inclined to chest or lung disorders are likely to find great alleviation from their problems. There is a risk of tiredness and incapacity as a result of over-exertion.

This is something you can easily avoid by not overworking yourself. When this is done, everything will be fine. This would also assist you in overcoming the potential of some nerve problems which might exist. Take care of yourself, and you will be in good health for the rest of the month. Pay more attention to the health of your teeth.

Travel

The horoscope from the stars doesn't tell us anything particularly favorable about travel. Writers, poets, and people like them may not have the best trips.

In fact, some of them could be seriously hurt by how unproductive their stays are.

You would travel alone, mostly by train or car, but you would also take a fair amount of flights. A trip abroad is also not out of the question. But it's not likely that these efforts would lead to even a holiday, which might not be all that fun. The best direction to go is South.

Insight from the stars

The energies of Sagittarius tend to make things hard for you. Stay quiet about your success and victory if you want to avoid these problems. Because life is short, make the most of it. During the 2023 Mercury retrograde, be careful not to overindulge so much that you hurt yourself or others.

Printed in Great Britain
by Amazon

16060269R00047